The Teddy Bears Picnic

A play by Janeen Brian

Illustrated by Susy Boyer

Series editor: Mark Carthew

**PEARSON
Longman**

Sydney, Melbourne, Brisbane and Perth

Characters

Toshi

Minnie
(Toshi's older sister)

Tim
(Toshi's older brother)

Papa

Mama

Nicki

Mr T
(Race Starter)

Stella

Ari

Jonah

Turn to page **21** for Sound and Stage Tips

The Teddy Bears Picnic

Scene 1 The Kitchen

(Minnie and Tim eat breakfast. Mama and Papa fold a picnic tablecloth.)

All: *(singing)* If you go down in the woods today, You're sure of a big …

Toshi: *(Enters carrying lots of toys.)* SURPRISE!

Mama: Toshi! What's all that stuff?

Toshi: I'm taking it to the picnic.

Papa: You can't take *all* that, Toshi.

Minnie: That's too much.

Toshi: *(sadly)* Can I take my trumpet then?

Mama: No.

Toshi: My train set?

Papa: No.

Toshi: My jigsaw?

Mama: No.

Toshi: My model plane.

Tim: No! Because that's mine!

(Tim takes the plane from Toshi.)

Toshi: Now I've got nothing to take but my ball.

Papa: That's okay. There are lots of other things to do at the Teddy Bears Picnic.

Minnie: *(Rubbing her tummy.)* Like eat!

Tim: And hide, Minnie, and chase each other.

Minnie: And play games, Tim, and have races too.

Mama: *(Picking up the basket.)* Come on, everyone. Let's go. We don't want to be late.

(They all set off out of the house and down a path.)

Toshi: Oh no!

All: What now, Toshi?

Toshi: I've forgotten something. Something *really* important. *(Running back inside and returning with his Teddy.)* Hey! Wait for me!

Scene 2   On the Path in the Woods

(Nicki, Ari, Jonah and Stella enter and approach the family.)

Minnie: Hi Nicki!

Tim: Hi Ari!

Nicki and Ari: Hi!

Toshi: Hi Jonah and Stella!

Jonah and Stella: Hi!

Mama: It's a lovely day for a walk in the woods, isn't it?

Nicki: Yes!

Papa: But we've still got a way to go to our picnic spot. Let's sing a song.

All: Hi ho, hi ho,
To a picnic we all go.
We'll have such fun
Out in the sun,
Hi ho, hi ho, hi ho, hi ho!

(They all march around in a large circle.)

Minnie: Hey! Look at that big tree.

Tim: Let's climb it.

All: Yes, let's!

Tim: We might be able to see the picnic spot.

Toshi: We might be able to see the whole world!

(They all mime climbing and waving to Mama and Papa.)

Papa: *(laughing)* Come on, all you monkeys! On we go!

(The Teddies mime climbing down. Toshi gets stuck and is the last to reach the ground.)

Toshi: *(Running after them.)* Hey! Wait for me!

Scene 3   In the Woods

(Mama and Papa sit down. The young Teddies start running around and playing leapfrog. Mr T blows the whistle.)

Sound FX: *(whistle)*

Mr T: Okay, Teddy-kids. It's time for the sack race. Everyone line up.

(The Teddies line up, holding onto their sacks.)

Toshi: Minnie?

Minnie: Yes?

Toshi: Is he going to blow that big whistle again?

Minnie: Yes. He has to blow it to start the race.

Toshi: I hate that noise. It's too loud.

Tim: Shh, Toshi. We won't hear when to start.

Toshi: But Tim, the whistle's too noisy. My ears don't like it!

Tim: Well, block them then.

(*Toshi puts his hands over his ears. Mr T blows the whistle.*)

Sound FX: (*whistle*)

(*Everyone starts jumping.*)

Toshi: (*Looking surprised.*) Hey, wait for me!

Toshi: *(Walking back after the race.)* I wish I was bigger, Teddy. I'm *always* last. No one waits for me.

(Toshi sits by a tree.)

Mr T: Okay, Teddy-kids! This time it's the running race. Everyone line up again.

(All the Teddies move to the starting line.)

Toshi: *(sadly)* I'm not going to go in this race, Teddy. Do you know why?

(He makes Teddy shake his head.)

Because I don't want to be last again. What? You've got an idea?

(Toshi holds Teddy up to his ear and smiles.)

That's a good idea, Teddy! Come on.

(Toshi lines up and blocks his ears. Mr T blows the whistle.

Sound FX: (whistle)

(Toshi unblocks his ears and starts running, then stops. The other Teddies finish the race.)

Toshi: Come on, everybody. You went the wrong way. You have to run back this way!

(The Teddies turn and run, but this time Toshi is in front.)

Hooray! I win!

(He laughs and jumps up and down.)

Tim: Well, all that running has made me hungry!

All: Me too! Me too!

Mama: Let's have our picnic. Toshi, would you like to go first?

Toshi: Yes please!

(All the Teddies exit except Mama and Papa.)

Scene 4   At the Picnic

(The picnic food is set out on the cloth. The Teddies walk in singing, each wearing a small disguise.)

All: If you go down in the woods today,
You're sure of a big surprise.
If you go down in the woods today,
You'd better go in disguise.

(On the word 'disguise' each Teddy takes off their disguise. They hold hands and dance around Toshi and the picnic food, singing the rest of the song.)

For ev'ry bear that ever there was
Will gather there for certain because
Today's the day
The Teddy Bears have their picnic!

(They all sit down in a circle.)

Papa: Have you had lots of fun so far?

All Teddies: Yes!

Minnie: Later we can play more games.

All Teddies: Yes!

Toshi: But let's eat first!

All Teddies: Yes! Yes! Yes!

Mama and Papa: What do we say first?

All Teddies: Two-four-six-eight. The Teddy Bears Picnic is just great!

(They punch their fists into the air, then reach for something to eat.)

Teddy Bears Picnic

If you go down in the woods today,
You're sure of a big surprise.
If you go down in the woods today,
You'd better go in disguise.
For ev'ry bear that ever there was
Will gather there for certain because
Today's the day
The Teddy Bears have their picnic!

Picnic time for Teddy Bears,
The little Teddy Bears
Are having a lovely time today.
Watch them, catch them unawares *(do not know)*
And see them picnic on their holiday.
See them gaily gad about, *(happily travel around to enjoy)*
They love to play and shout,
They never have any cares.
At six o'clock their mummies and daddies
Will take them home to bed
Because they're tired little Teddy Bears.

Sound and Stage Tips

About This Play

This play is a story you can read with your friends in a group or act out in front of an audience. Before you start reading, choose a part or parts you would like to read or act. There are ten main parts in this play, so make sure you have readers for all the parts. You may wish to have a group of students play the roles of other Teddy Bears.

Reading This Play

It's a good idea to read the play through to yourself before you read it as part of a group. It is best to have your own book, as that will help you too. As you read the play through, think about each character and how they might look and sound. How are they behaving? What sort of voice might they have?

Rehearsing the Play

Rehearse the play a few times before you perform it for others. In *The Teddy Bears Picnic*, it is fun to shout and cry out during the games and races.

Remember you are an actor as well as a reader. Your facial expressions and the way you move your body will really help the play to come alive!

Using Your Voice

Remember to speak out clearly and be careful not to read too quickly! Speak more slowly than you do when you're speaking to your friends. Keep in mind that the audience is hearing your words for the first time.

The songs in *The Teddy Bears Picnic* are great fun to sing and perform. Remember to look at the audience and at the other actors, making sure everyone can hear what you are saying.

Creating Sound Effects (FX)

You may like to add music to the songs. You could use percussion or other musical instruments. You could even play a tape or CD of the 'The Teddy Bears Picnic' song.

Sets and Props

Once you have read the play, make a list of the things you will need. Here are some ideas to help your performance. You may like to add some of your own.

- Table and chairs for the kitchen scene
- Trumpet, train set, jigsaw, model plane, ball and teddy for Toshi
- Picnic basket
- Picnic tablecloth and food
- Cardboard trees and bushes for the picnic scene

- Tree to climb (it could be a ladder with a cut-out of a tree placed in front)
- Whistle
- Sacks
- Small disguises for each Teddy, such as sunglasses, a party hat or a false nose

Costumes

This play can be performed with or without costumes. If you wish to dress up, you may find the following useful.

- Teddy Bear masks (or face paint) and ears
- Furry jumpers

Have fun!

When she was young, Janeen Brian would hang a sheet over the vine trellis, as a curtain for the plays she made up on the back lawn. She always liked telling stories at lunchtime too. Janeen likes to write things that make her laugh, but she mainly just loves words.

Janeen has many other loves in her life too. Her daughters, Natalie and Cassie, and her partner, Jon, her dog, trees, nature, making mosaics, the beach, exercising, Adelaide in South Australia (where she lives) and reading with a capital 'R'!